YOU AND SCHOOL

A SURVIVAL GUIDE FOR ADOLESCENCE

By Gail C. Roberts, B.Ed., M.A.
and Lorraine Guttormson, M.A.

Edited by Rosemary Wallner

free
Spirit ®
PUBLISHING

10 9 8 7 6 5 4 3

Printed in the United States of America

Cover and book design by MacLean & Tuminelly

Supervising editor: Pamela Espeland

Free Spirit Publishing Inc.
400 First Avenue North, Suite 616
Minneapolis, MN 55401
(612) 338-2068

CONTENTS

INTRODUCTION

You and School: A Survival Guide for Adolescence has been designed for you, with respect for your uniqueness and your potential. Working through it won't always be easy. The activities call upon you to be honest with yourself, to be open to new ideas, and to be willing to grow.

We hope the activities will lead you to some exciting discoveries about yourself and the world around you. We hope they will help you to understand and accept yourself, and to become more understanding and accepting of others. We hope they will give you a sense of having some degree of control over your life, and ultimately free you to be the best person you can be.

Gail C. Roberts, B.Ed., M.A.
Lorraine Guttormson, M.A.
August 1990

LEARNING IN AND OUT OF SCHOOL

You learn something new almost every day.
There are two types of learning: *formal education* and *informal education*.

At school, you get a formal education as you learn how to spell new words, solve new math problems, do science experiments, and research history facts. You study the subjects your Department of Education requires for students in your grade. Your formal education might also include things like music lessons, art classes, foreign language classes, or special coaching you get from an instructor over a period of time.

You get an informal education by learning something on your own, or learning through living. Your informal education includes skills like learning how to make friends, handle more freedom, cope with limitations, set personal goals, and achieve your goals.

Throughout your life, you will continue to learn. Each stage of life has informal lessons to teach you. And even when you're out of school, you may choose to take classes at any age to continue your formal education. You will always be learning something new.

ACTIVITY 1

Fill in these charts
with examples of
the new skills you
hope to master in
the future.

Next week

Formal	Informal

Next month

Formal	Informal

Next year

Formal	Informal

In five years

Formal	Informal

In ten years

Formal	Informal

In twenty years

Formal	Informal

In forty years

Formal	Informal

In sixty years

Formal	Informal

ACTIVITY 2

YOUR LIKES AND DISLIKES ABOUT SCHOOL

As part of your formal education, you go to school. Your school may be large or small, in the city or in the country. You might walk to school or you might ride a bus. You may learn on computers or discuss topics in groups. You may have one teacher or you may have many different teachers.

What do you like MOST about your school?

1. _____

2. _____

3. _____

4. _____

5. _____

What do you like LEAST about your school?

1. _____

2. _____

3. _____

4. _____

5. _____

WHY ARE THERE SCHOOLS?

Different people have different ideas about why there are schools. Why do YOU think there are schools? List as many reasons as you can.

1. _____

2. _____

3. _____

4. _____

5. _____

6. _____

7. _____

8. _____

9. _____

10. _____

ACTIVITY 3

Did you think of these?

How many of these reasons did you think of for why there are schools?

• At school, you learn about other people's ideas. School is where you begin to learn about the world.

• At school, you can learn about subjects that interest you. You can learn about rockets, horses, explorers, or aquariums.

• During school field trips, you can visit a museum, go backstage at a theater, or tour a factory.

• At school, you learn how to get along with other people.

• At school, you learn the traditions and values of your society.

• Schools let you do many different activities. You can act in a play, join a team, write poems, or learn to play a musical instrument.

• Schools teach you knowledge and skills which help you to make your way in the world.

WHY DO *YOU* GO TO SCHOOL?

There may be many reasons why you go to school. Number the reasons on pages 7 and 8 in order of how important they are to you. Put a 1 by the most important reason why you go to school. Put a 2 by the second most important reason, and so on. Add your own reasons and number them, too.

NOTE: Some of you may get your formal education at home. Maybe you take correspondence courses or TV or video classes. Maybe a tutor comes to your house, or your parents teach you. This still counts as "going to school."

I go to school because…

____ I want to learn how to think

____ I want to get a general education

____ I like to learn

____ all my friends are there

____ I want to get training for a future job or career

____ I like school

____ I have to go—it's the law

____ I like the extracurricular (after school) activities

ACTIVITY 4

____ my parents make me go

____ it's better than being at home or on the street

____ _____

____ _____

____ _____

Something to think about

Does a person have to "learn how to learn"?
If yes, what does this involve?

SCHOOL ATTENDANCE

Why do schools keep a close eye on where students are during the day? It's because they are *legally responsible* for you when your parents or guardians aren't around.

You are at school for a certain number of hours each day. During those hours, your school is responsible for your safety, actions, and whereabouts. That's why there are always adults around during recess, lunchtime, on field trips, and during extracurricular activities. And that's why you need an excuse whenever you are late or absent.

A student who stays away from school without a reasonable excuse is called a *truant*. Truancy is a crime. If an underage child is truant, the parents or guardians are held legally responsible. Sometimes parents or guardians are fined by the court for failing to make sure that their children attend school regularly.

ACTIVITY 5

Have you ever told a lie or made up a story about why you were late for school? YES ☐ NO ☐

If YES, answer these questions:

• What was the lie or story you told?

_____

_____

• Why did you tell this lie or story?

_____

_____

• Did your teacher believe you? YES ☐ NO ☐

• If your teacher DID believe you, why? If your teacher DIDN'T believe you, why not?

_____

_____

• Did your parent believe you? YES ☐ NO ☐

• If your parent DID believe you, why? If your parent DIDN'T believe you, why not?

_____

_____

• What were the consequences of the lie or story you told?

_____

_____

• Have you told a lie or made up a story about being late more than once? YES ☐ NO ☐

Have you ever told a lie or made up a story about why you were absent from school? YES ☐ NO ☐

If YES, answer these questions:

• What was the lie or story you told?

_____

_____

• Why did you tell this lie or story?

_____

_____

• Did your teacher believe you? YES ☐ NO ☐

• If your teacher DID believe you, why? If your teacher DIDN'T believe you, why not?

_____

_____

• Did your parent believe you? YES ☐ NO ☐

• If your parent DID believe you, why? If your parent DIDN'T believe you, why not?

_____

_____

• What were the consequences of the lie or story you told?

_____

_____

• Have you told a lie or made up a story about being absent more than once? YES ☐ NO ☐

_____

_____

EXCUSES, EXCUSES

"The work is boring." "I hate the teacher." "I'd rather watch TV." "The other kids tease me." These are just a few of the excuses students give for being late or absent from school.

Brainstorm more excuses. Come up with as many as you can.

1. _____

2. _____

3. _____

4. _____

5. _____

6. _____

7. _____

8. _____

9. _____

10. _____

Which of these excuses do you think your teacher or principal would accept?

_____

_____

_____

A teacher may react very differently to two students who give the same excuse. Why do you think this happens?

_____

_____

_____

If people or events in your life are keeping you from going to school, you can get help. Talk to the school counselor, your teacher, the principal, or the school social worker. Is there anyone else you can think of?

ACTIVITY 7

TRUANCY AND THE LAW

There are laws that define truancy and spell out what should be done if a student is truant. To answer these questions, you'll need to find out about the laws in your area. Start by asking your teacher or principal. Ask to see a copy of your school's handbook and look up the rules about truancy. Books in the library will also help you to complete this section.

1. What does the law say is a *reasonable* excuse for a student to be absent from school?

_____

_____

_____

2. What happens at your school when a student is truant? In other words, what are the consequences of being truant?

_____

_____

_____

3. Does your school have a person on staff whose job is to prevent truancy and enforce the consequences of being truant? (This person might be called an "attendance officer.") YES ☐ NO ☐

4. How old do you have to be before you legally can quit school?

_____

It's usually against the law to drop out of school until you reach a certain age. But sometimes the law lets a student quit school early, with parental permission. For example, the student might be needed to help a disabled family member, or to go to work.

Dropping out of school is a very serious thing to do. Not having a diploma quickly limits your options. You may find that the jobs you are qualified for pay the minimum wage. This may seem like enough for now, but it may not be if you decide one day to have a family or buy a home.

Many dropouts discover that they need better skills and qualifications if they want to keep a job, get a promotion, get a better job, or start a new line of work. They often wish they had stayed in school when they had the chance. They may decide to go to night school, summer school, or Saturday school to make up for what they missed. They may take correspondence courses on their own. Learning takes a lot longer when you do it for many short periods of time instead of full-time. And it can be a lot harder when you don't have a teacher nearby to help.

If you ever think about dropping out, be sure to talk to several adults first—adults whose opinions you trust and respect. And be prepared to return to school at some time in the future—you probably will have to!

ACTIVITY 8

LEARNING ABOUT YOUR PARENTS

Do you know what your parents' education means to them? Use these questions to interview your parents and other adults about their education. Try to interview a variety of people with different educational backgrounds.

Some adults may feel uncomfortable talking about their education. If they don't want to answer some or all of these questions, respect their feelings.

Do you think you had too much, too little, or just enough formal education? Give some reasons for your answer.

Adult #1 _____

_____

Adult #2 _____

_____

Adult #3 _____

_____

What are some ways you have used your formal education in your life?

Adult #1 _____

_____

Adult #2 _____

_____

Adult #3 _____

_____

What is the most important thing you ever learned in school?

Adult #1 _____

_____

Adult #2 _____

_____

Adult #3 _____

_____

What is the most important thing you ever learned in life?

Adult #1 _____

_____

Adult #2 _____

_____

Adult #3 _____

_____

ACTIVITY 8

Are you continuing your formal education in any way? For example, are you going to night school or summer school, or taking correspondence courses?

Adult #1 _____

_____

Adult #2 _____

_____

Adult #3 _____

_____

What are some other ways in which you are continuing to learn?

Adult #1 _____

_____

Adult #2 _____

_____

Adult #3 _____

_____

Something to think about

When you were doing these interviews, did you learn anything that changed your own attitudes or opinions about education?

AN EDUCATION QUIZ

Take this Education Quiz to learn more about schools and students in your area. You may need to do some research to find the answers. Ask your teacher or principal, visit your public library, or contact your Department of Education.

1. How many students are enrolled in schools in your area? _____
In your country? _____

2. What is the average age of students in your area? _____
In your grade? _____

3. Which grade has the most students? _____

4. On average, how much money is spent on each student in your area per year? _____

5. What is the percentage of dropouts in your area? _____
In your country? _____

6. How old does a student in your area have to be before he or she legally may quit school? _____

7. How much education did your teacher complete before being hired to work at your school? _____

How much education did your principal complete before being hired to work at your school? _____

8. What high schools are in your area?

_____

_____

9. What colleges or universities are in your area?

_____

_____

10. What vocational training schools are in your area?

_____

_____

11. What is the percentage of students in your area who finish high school? _____ How does this compare to your nation's average? ☐MORE students in my area finish high school than the national average ☐FEWER students in my area finish high school than the national average ☐The two are about the same

12. What is the percentage of students in your area who finish college or vocational training? _____ How does this compare to your nation's average? ☐MORE students in my area finish college or vocational training than the national average ☐FEWER students in my area finish college or vocational training than the national average ☐The two are about the same

WHAT MAKES A SCHOOL "GOOD" OR "BAD"?

Do you go to a "good" school or a "bad" school? Some people define a "good" school as one where students get high scores on standardized tests, or the basketball team takes the championship. Some people define a "bad" school as one where there are problems with crime, drugs, and high dropout rates. But most people agree that a "good" school is one where a student can get the best education possible.

There are many things that determine whether a school is "good" or "bad." Here are just a few:

• the attitudes and behavior of the students

• how involved parents are in volunteering, going to conferences, helping their children with homework, and other activities that support the school

• donations from the community to the school of time, energy, talent, money, equipment, and other necessities

• how dedicated and committed the teachers and administrators are

• class size, and the student-teacher ratio

• the size of the school budget

• whether the school offers special programs (like the ones listed on pages 22–24)

• whether the school offers extracurricular activities (like sports and clubs)

ACTIVITY 10

- staff turnover (how often teachers and administrators leave and are replaced by others new to the school)

- the age of the building and how well it is maintained

Everybody looks for something different in a school. Some people look for computers, video equipment, and "media labs" as proof that a school is up-to-date with technology. Other people want small class sizes. Others want to know how many graduates go on to college, or whether the school offers wide a variety of courses to choose from. Still others want a school to emphasize athletics, religious instruction, or fine arts.

Think about your school, then answer these questions. Ask your teacher to help you with the ones you can't answer.

What regular courses or subjects does your school offer?

_____

_____

_____

_____

_____

_____

_____

_____

_____

_____

_____

Does your school offer any special courses or programs? Read this list of possibilities. Put a check mark by each one that's offered by your school. If you know about others, add them to the list.

____ classes in foreign languages such as French, Spanish, or Japanese

____ classes in English as a second language

____ enrichment or honors programs for bright or gifted students

_____ support programs for students with learning disabilities

_____ support programs for students with emotional disabilities

_____ special interest programs such as band, art, or computer science

_____ vocational programs such as hair styling, automotive, or computer repair

_____ extracurricular sports

_____ a school newspaper or yearbook that students can work on

_____ special interest clubs such as chess club, computer club, or folk dancing club

_____ reading and communications skills programs

_____ parent or community volunteer programs

_____ a peer tutoring program

_____ visits from a dentist or dental assistant

_____ a sex education program

_____ a program for unwed parents

_____ a family life program

_____ a study skills program

_____ police community service programs

_____ a testing program for hearing and sight

_____ a vaccination program

_____ regular visits from a public health professional

_____ career education programs

_____ drug and alcohol abuse programs

_____ a hot lunch program

_____ a before-and-after-school child care program ("latch key")

_____ a personal safety program

____ summer school

____ _____

____ _____

____ _____

____ _____

Now go back and put a second check mark by the programs YOU have participated in. If there are others you would like to try, who can you talk to about arranging this?

Does your school have any special support people on staff? Read this list of possibilities. Put a check mark by each person who works at your school, either part-time or full-time. If you know about others, add them to the list.

____ a guidance counselor

____ a social worker

____ a physiotherapist (someone who does therapy with students who have physical disabilities)

____ a reading specialist

____ a music specialist

____ an art specialist

____ a computer specialist

____ a speech and hearing therapist

____ a peace officer

____ _____

____ _____

____ _____

____ _____

Now go back and put a second check mark by the people YOU have worked with or learned from. If there are others you would like to get to know, who can you talk to about arranging this?

PUBLIC SCHOOLS AND PRIVATE SCHOOLS

Most students attend *public schools.* These schools are tuition free to everyone because they are supported by taxes. And almost everyone can get into public school. Many parents believe that public schools offer the best education and the best chance for their kids to learn about other people and cultures.

Some students attend *private schools.* These schools charge fees for tuition, and also for room and board if students live there. Some receive financial support from donations, government funding, and churches. Not everyone can get into private school. Many private schools have entrance requirements. Some are too expensive for most families. If you want to attend a private school, you may be able to earn a scholarship to help pay the tuition.

Some private schools are associated with religious groups. Some are only for girls, while others are only for boys. Private schools may require their students to buy and wear uniforms. They may require students to study specific subjects, or to participate in specific extracurricular activities.

If you attend a public school…

1. What do you know about private schools?

_____

_____

_____

2. What do you think would be some advantages of attending a private school?

_____

_____

_____

3. What do you think would be some disadvantages of attending a private school?

_____

_____

_____

If you attend a private school...

1. What do you know about public schools?

_____

_____

_____

2. What do you think would be some advantages of attending a public school?

_____

_____

_____

3. What do you think would be some disadvantages of attending a public school?

_____

_____

_____

HOME SCHOOLING

Many parents choose to educate their children at home instead of sending them to a school. This is often called "home schooling."

These parents must meet specific government requirements. They must prove to the Department of Education that their children are being educated at or above the grade level they would be in if they went to a regular school. They must use teaching materials that have been approved by the Department of Education.

Think about home schooling. What are some reasons why parents might decide to educate their children at home?

_____

_____

_____

_____

_____

_____

_____

_____

ACTIVITY 12

Did you think of these?

How many of these reasons did you think of for parents to choose home schooling for their children?

- The family may live in a remote area where there is no school.

- The parents may be temporarily living in a foreign country where there are no English-language schools available.

- The family may travel or move frequently.

- A certified teacher (perhaps your parent, a relative, or a friend) may agree to instruct the children at home.

- A child may be sick at home for a long period of time and unable to attend school.

- The parents may believe that home schooling would give their children a better education.

- The parents may be unhappy with the schools in the area.

- The family may practice a religion that they believe should be part of the children's everyday education.

- A child may be a movie or TV actor, a model, a circus performer, an apprentice in a special field, or someone who is working full time.

Something to think about

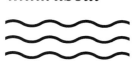

What are some advantages to home schooling? What are some disadvantages?

School Structures and Systems

Imagine that a teacher wants to change a school policy. Before the teacher can do this, he or she must tell the principal. If the change is an important one, the principal must report it to his or her superiors. Then these people must talk the change over with *their* superiors. And so on, until most people connected with the school have had a say in what should or shouldn't be changed.

Where do *you* fit into your school's chain of command? As you can see, many people are available to support you and your school.

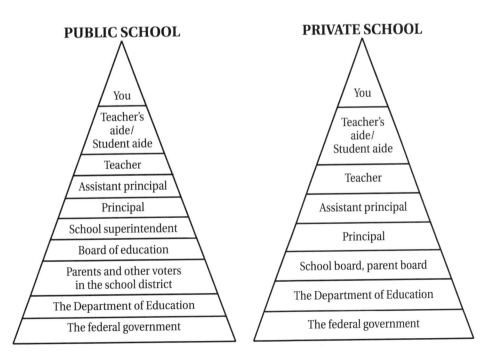

PUBLIC SCHOOL

- You
- Teacher's aide/ Student aide
- Teacher
- Assistant principal
- Principal
- School superintendent
- Board of education
- Parents and other voters in the school district
- The Department of Education
- The federal government

PRIVATE SCHOOL

- You
- Teacher's aide/ Student aide
- Teacher
- Assistant principal
- Principal
- School board, parent board
- The Department of Education
- The federal government

ACTIVITY 13

Ask your teacher or principal how your school is organized. Draw a diagram of your school's chain of decision-making. Put yourself at the top of the triangle—your school exists to meet *your* needs.

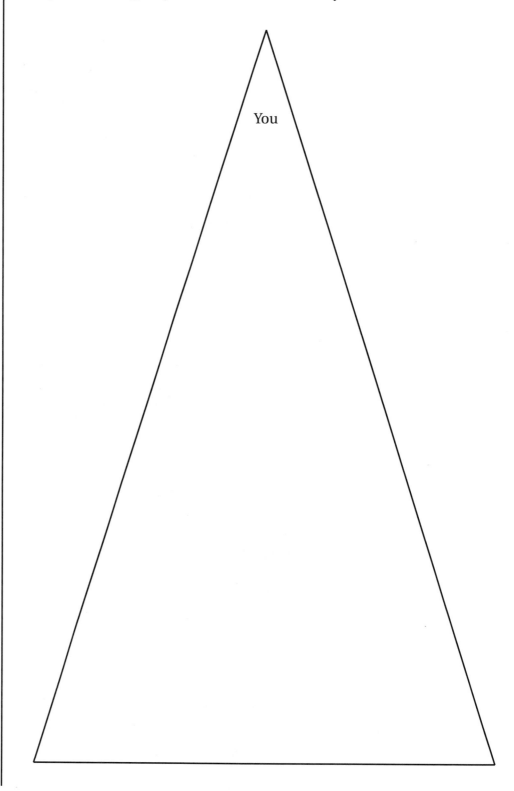

You

TRANSFERRING

Transferring means leaving one school to enroll in another. Students transfer because their families move to another city, or because they want to attend a different school in their own city.

1

Have you ever transferred? YES ☐ NO ☐

If YES, answer these questions. (If NO, move on to question #2.)

• Why did you transfer?

_____

_____

_____

• In what ways was this a positive experience?

_____

_____

• In what ways was this a negative experience?

_____

_____

• How could this have been a better experience?

_____

_____

ACTIVITY 14

• Are you settled into your new school? YES ☐ NO ☐

• If YES, how long did it take to get used to your new classmates, new teachers, and new routine?

_____

• Are you happy with the change you made? YES ☐ NO ☐

• Why or why not?

_____

_____

If you have never transferred, answer these questions:

• Would you choose to transfer, if you could? YES ☐ NO ☐

• What school would you transfer to?

_____

• Why would you pick that school?

_____

_____

• Have you ever talked to your parents or teachers about this? YES ☐ NO ☐

Something to think about

Students who transfer schools usually take their records and grades from their old school to their new school. They might also ask their old teachers and principal to write letters of introduction to their new teachers and principal. This may make it easier for them to adjust to a new school.

TEACHER TYPES

People tend to classify one another into groups—young people and old people, rich and poor, male and female, black and white, tall and short, of one nationality or religion or another. They tend to assume that all of the people within a particular group have certain qualities. When they exaggerate or fix those qualities in their minds, they *stereotype* the people in that group.

For example, a poor person may think that *all* rich people are snobs. Or a rich person may think that *all* poor people are lazy. An elderly person may think that *all* teenagers are delinquents. A teenager may think that *all* elderly people are boring. A woman truck driver may think that *all* doctors are men who play golf during office hours. A woman doctor may think that *all* truck drivers are men who attend wrestling matches on their days off. A male nurse may think that *all* ballet dancers are moody and temperamental. A male dancer may think that *all* nurses are female. What's wrong with such *stereotypic thinking?*

Our world is full of stereotypes. For example, advertisements often portray homemakers as women who don't care about anything besides clean floors and clean clothes. Comic strips often portray athletes as "all muscle and no brains," or children as "know-it-alls" who easily manipulate adults. Situation comedies often portray apartment managers as nosy, lawyers as sly, employers as bossy, fathers as not knowing what's going on in their families, and so on. What other examples of "humorous stereotyping" do you know about?

How do you react when someone stereotypes you? Or, if you think this has never happened, how would you react if it did?

ACTIVITY 15

People are most likely to stereotype those who look different from themselves, who act in ways they don't understand, or who cause them to feel insecure or afraid. When they think that *all* members of a particular group have negative qualities, or even *one* member has those qualities, serious misunderstandings and problems may arise. What examples of "harmful stereotyping" do you know about?

You've probably met many different teachers over the years. For the most part, teachers are dedicated, hardworking professionals who make a sincere effort to help all of their students. Although the majority of teachers are good instructors, this activity focuses on teachers you may find it hard to learn from. Read each description, then draw a *humorous*—not hurtful—cartoon of that "teacher type." This will give you practice in handling difficult situations with humor.

The classic blackboard cartoon

While you are drawing your cartoons, remember that teachers have feelings, too. Like you, they have unique strengths and weaknesses, big and little problems, good and bad days. Don't put the name of a real person on **any** of your drawings.

**THE ONE
WHO PLAYS
FAVORITES**

…favors some of the kids in class, usually the ones most like him or her

…may not be a very good instructor, but most kids don't care because he or she is so attractive and charming

…may not be respected by the other teachers

…may find that students compete for his or her attention—most students want this teacher to like them

Coping Tips:

• Participate actively in class discussions.

• Stick up for yourself; you don't have to put yourself down to gain anyone's favor.

• Try to understand and appreciate the teacher's extracurricular activities, interests, and enthusiasms.

• Don't criticize the "teacher's pets." They may feel awkward enough already, or they may not know what to do when they fall out of favor or get a teacher who doesn't play favorites.

ACTIVITY 15

THE TIME SERVER

...isn't really interested in school, in teaching, or in the students

...seldom instructs, assigns, or grades anything

...may let the class misbehave or do nothing

...may use class time to pursue personal interests

Coping Tips:

• Design a project, write an essay, or do some extra work to show that you are eager to learn. Then ask the teacher to guide you.

• Take responsibility for teaching yourself. Read the materials anyway, do the homework, and read related materials from the library.

• Never take advantage of the situation by misbehaving or being lazy.

• Talk this over with your parents. Ask for their advice. Maybe you can go together to meet with the teacher and the principal and explain the situation to them. *You have the right to a good education.*

DR.
EDUCATION

...is always right, no matter what

...is unbending about rules and very strict about details

...knows a subject so well and loves it so much that he or she may not be able to understand why you are having trouble with the material, or why the subject does not interest you

...may forget that you have other subjects to study for; gives unrealistic amounts of homework and tests

Coping Tips:

• Try to respect the teacher's knowledge.

• Learn as much as you can by doing your homework and taking notes in class.

• If you are feeling burdened or stressed out because of the workload, arrange to talk with your teacher privately. Explain the situation to him or her. See if you can work out a compromise, a time extension, or some other arrangement. Then live up to your part of the bargain!

• If the teacher won't listen to you, talk to the school counselor or the principal, with your parents.

ACTIVITY 15

**NO FRILLS,
NO FANCY
STUFF**

...always follows the rules and the curriculum to the letter

...moves at a regular, steady pace through the course, whether the work is hard or easy

...is not particularly interesting, enthusiastic, or creative, but is calm, fair, and has common sense

...is predictable, but often boring

Coping Tips:

• Try to make the course more interesting for yourself. Ask questions in class. Read other books about the subject. Research related ideas. Design and do an independent project. Offer to become an expert and do a class presentation. Find a guest speaker or a film that would help to make the subject more interesting. Suggest a class field trip.

• Remember that this class won't last forever. Just make the best of it.

THE IDEALIST

...is devoted to the students

...lives for teaching

...expects you always to do your very best in his or her class

...is hopeful, helpful, and encouraging and won't allow you to be cautious, to go slow, or to express worries or concerns

Coping Tips:

• If you don't share your teacher's idealism, don't make fun of it. That teaching style may be just what other students need.

• Try to meet the teacher's expectations—do your best in class. You may surprise yourself.

• Make the most of your teacher's hopeful, helpful, encouraging qualities. This could be one of your *best* classes ever...*if* you loosen up a little and let your imagination go.

ACTIVITY 15

THE LEMON

...may be rude and sarcastic at times

...may be moody and unfair

...may be feared, even hated by students

Coping Tips:

• Try being especially pleasant, cooperative, and hardworking. Being rude and sarcastic can only make things worse.

• Talk privately to this teacher to see if there's something specific you can do to make the classroom a better place. Sometimes this type of teacher is dealing with very difficult health or personal problems.

• If you feel that the teacher's attitude is keeping you from learning, tell your parents or other adults you trust. Get help.

THE SHARER

...wants to learn along with the students in a process of mutual discovery

...is unpredictable and spontaneous; may seem to be unfocused or disorganized

...may not want to give simple "yes" or "no" answers to questions

...may not give clear instructions or firm assignment deadlines

Coping Tips:

• Ask questions in class to show your interest in the subject. Ask questions that will help to make clear what is expected of you.

• Be a sharer. Bring your ideas and experiences into the classroom.

• Take the initiative. Ask to borrow extra materials. Do extra research at the library.

• If the teacher's spontaneous, disorganized ways bother you, try to get him or her back on topic by asking specific questions. Or ask the teacher to give you a specific example or a demonstration.

• If you need more organization, definite due dates, and concrete, sequential instruction, ask for them—politely.

ACTIVITY 15

THE SPECIAL ONE

…may be a truly unique individual who has a wonderful outlook on life or approach to life—someone so amazing and rare that you don't know how to react to him or her

…may be a different race, religion, age, or in different physical condition than most of the other teachers

…may have a serious problem, such as financial worries, ill health, or family or psychological problems

…may have expectations and use teaching methods you have never experienced before

Coping Tips:

• Talk to this teacher. Explain your confusion.

• Find out what makes your teacher special. This can be a great learning opportunity for you. For example, if he or she is from another country, learn everything you can about his or her culture. If the teacher has one or more disabilities, learn to understand him or her instead of making fun of the difference. If the teacher has a special talent—as an artist, storyteller, musician, or something else—take this opportunity to develop your own talent in that area, if this interests you. Your teacher can be your *mentor*—someone who helps you learn by example and support.

??????????

Do you know another "teacher type"? Write a description. Draw a picture. Come up with some coping tips of your own.

_____

_____

_____

Coping Tips:

_____

_____

_____

STUDENT TYPES

Just as you probably have met many different teachers, you probably have had a wide variety of classmates. And you probably have learned a great deal from them, both formally and informally.

This activity focuses on classmates who may interfere with your formal learning. Read each description, then draw a *humorous* — not hurtful — cartoon of that "student type." This will give you practice in handling difficult situations with humor.

While you are drawing each cartoon, be sure to think about how it might affect someone who recognizes himself or herself in it. How would *you* feel if someone drew a cartoon of you? If someone drew an especially hurtful cartoon of you? Let kindness, humor, and good will guide your pencil. Don't put the name of a real person on any of your drawings.

THE SOCIAL BUTTERFLY

…dresses in the latest styles

…passes notes in class

…can't wait to get home from school to call friends on the telephone

…"collects" other social butterflies as friends

…is always talking

Coping Tips:

• To be liked by this person is to be included; to be disliked by this person is to be excluded. There are certain things you may have to do to get and keep his or her friendship. Decide if it's worth it to do these things.

• A harmless social butterfly is lively and fun to be around. Enjoy!

• A harmful social butterfly can be a real trouble-maker. Beware!

ACTIVITY 16

THE SLEEPER

...has no interest in school

...may daydream or fall asleep in class

...usually doesn't do very well in school

...is often late to school because he or she has overslept

...is often absent

Coping Tips:

• This person may be interesting to know. Maybe he or she has family or work responsibilities that prevent him or her from getting enough sleep. Maybe he or she is unwell.

• You may want to alert the teacher to this student's situation, if the teacher doesn't seem to notice.

• If this person's snoring (or indifference to learning) distracts you, explain this to the teacher and ask to be moved elsewhere in the room.

• If this person is assigned to be your partner on a project and turns out to be unreliable or unhelpful, explain this to the teacher well before the assignment is due. Ask to be reassigned to another partner, or ask to work alone.

THE SUPER STUDENT

…has read every textbook and the whole school library

…knows the answer before the teacher even asks the question

…may think that he or she knows more than the teacher

…may act bored in class

Coping Tips:

• Try not to be intimidated by this person. He or she is human, too.

• If the other students tease or make fun of this academically gifted or talented student, don't join in.

• You may want to ask this person to tutor you. What could you do to return the favor?

• The academically gifted and talented student may *seem* self-sufficient, but he or she may be lonely (and not even know it). Try being friendly for several weeks and see what happens.

ACTIVITY 16

THE JOCK

...has a talent for many sports

...may be outgoing and confident

...may have good leadership qualities

...may be perceived as "dumb," even if he or she is an average or good student

Coping Tips:

• If you aren't a "team person," experiment with individual sports like tennis, golf, archery, and gymnastics.

• If you have one or more physical disabilities, you can still participate in sports and games. Maybe the activities can be modified or the rules changed slightly. Maybe you can take part by learning to be a time keeper, a score keeper, or a record keeper.

• A jock may admire (and sometimes even envy) a top student, a good public speaker, a fine musician, or a responsible person who has to go home after school to care for family members. Share your talents and, if you feel like it, explain your reasons for not being involved in sports.

THE CLASS CLOWN

...shows off, even if there's a good chance of getting in trouble

...can make even the teacher laugh, but usually drives teachers crazy

...is always trying to get attention

...may be uncooperative and disruptive in class

...may have a group of followers

Coping Tips:

• Recognize that this person needs a lot of attention. Maybe he or she doesn't get enough at home. Or maybe he or she *does* get a lot of attention at home, so expects it everywhere.

• If this person distracts and annoys you, take him or her aside and explain (as kindly as you can) why doing well in school is important to you. He or she may not care, but at least you tried. On the other hand, he or she may respect your views and treat you accordingly.

• If you are tempted to follow this person and be a "clown" yourself, ask your teacher to give you five good reasons why you shouldn't. Write them down and tape them inside your notebook. When you are tempted to misbehave or act irresponsibly in school, read your list of reasons not to.

THE TEACHER'S PET

...tries very hard to please the teacher

...is always prepared for class

...usually asks for extra help

...always volunteers to help the teacher

Coping Tips:

• Remember that some students are more comfortable with adults and their ways than with their peers. They may like the rewards adults can give, or fear their punishments.

• The "teacher's pet" may be expected to behave this way at home, and may not see his or her behavior as unusual or offensive to other students.

• You may try to be more like this student yourself, or you may try to explain (politely) how his or her behavior makes you feel.

THE EXPERT

…excels in one area only (which may or may not be school-related)

…may be a "mad scientist," a disc jockey, a computer wizard, or a poet

…may talk endlessly about his or her special interest

…may make others feel that what they do or know is unimportant

Coping Tips:

• You may be interested in the same thing as the expert — or decide to develop an interest in it. Share what you know, and learn from him or her.

• Do a project together to widen your knowledge and enhance your ability to cooperate.

ACTIVITY 16

THE SLOW ONE

…may have trouble grasping new concepts

…may have to practice something over and over again to get it right

…may give up easily

…may have a poor memory for academic subjects

Coping Tips:

• Remember that no one chooses to be "the slow one." Like being born with a healthy body, being born with the ability to learn easily is largely a matter of luck. Not all people are lucky.

• Recognize that some people who don't do well at school work are very often good at other things — for example, at caring for plants or animals, at fixing machines, or at cooking.

• Some people who *seem* slow may need help with the English language before studying other subjects. You may want to help them.

• Many people who were told they would never amount to anything because they were slow at learning turned out to be very successful. Some examples: Albert Einstein, Thomas Edison, Winston Churchill, and Helen Keller.

• Use your relationship with this special person to develop your patience, your compassion, and your appreciation of individual differences.

THE TOUGH

...looks and acts aggressive

...may be rude, sarcastic, and uncooperative in class

...may be feared by other students, even some teachers

...may feel peer pressure from other "toughs" to do things he or she doesn't want to do, or may be a gang member by choice

Coping Tips:

• Sometimes toughs just need someone to be kind to them. Determine if this person is all bark and no bite, some bark and some bite, or no bark and all bite.

• You don't have to share space with a classmate who truly frightens you. Talk to the teacher, the principal, your parents — whoever can help to change this situation for you.

ACTIVITY 16

THE SPECIAL ONE

...may be a truly unique individual who has a wonderful outlook on life or approach to life — someone so amazing and rare that you don't know how to react to him or her

...may be a different race, religion, age, or physical condition than most of the other students

...may have one or more serious problems, such as financial worries, ill health, or family or psychological problems

Coping Tips:

• Talk to this person. Explain your confusion.

• Find out what makes this person special. This can be a wonderful learning opportunity for you. For example, if the person is from another country, learn everything you can about his or her culture. If the person has one or more disabilities, learn to understand him or her instead of making fun of the difference. If the person has a special talent, take this opportunity to develop your own talent in that area, if this interests you.

THE O.K. KID

…works at an acceptable level and has acceptable success in school

…does what is expected of him or her, most of the time

…is good in some subjects, weak in others

Coping Tips:

• Most of us don't need help coping with so-called "ordinary" people. We just need to decide for ourselves if *we* are satisfied with being "ordinary."

• Psychologists say that our brains are like icebergs — 90 percent submerged. That is, most of us use only 10 percent of our thinking capacity.

How can you learn to use more of your brain power? By deliberately *practicing* thinking skills. You will find descriptions of some thinking skills on pages 62–63 of Activity #17: What Kind of Student Are You?

ACTIVITY 16

YOU

What "type" of student are you? Maybe you're one of the types described in this activity — or maybe you're not. Write a description of yourself or draw a self-portrait. Think about how *you* affect your classmates' formal learning. Come up with some coping tips to help other students deal with your type.

_____

_____

Coping Tips:

_____

_____

Does the "type" of student you are affect how teachers treat you? Does it affect how other students react to you?

Something to think about

56

WHAT KIND OF STUDENT ARE YOU?

Do you consider yourself to be a good student? If not, would you like to be a good student?

In most cases, being a good student takes a combination of the right attitude, specific habits, and certain skills. To find out about your attitude, habits, and skills, answer these questions as honestly as you can. For each, put a check mark by "very often," "sometimes," or "never." You will figure out your score at the end, *after* you answer all of the questions.

MY SCORE

1. How often do you bring books, paper, and pens to class?

VERY OFTEN____ SOMETIMES____ NEVER____

2. How often do you remember that teachers are people, too?

VERY OFTEN____ SOMETIMES____ NEVER____

3. How often do you arrive on time to class?

VERY OFTEN____ SOMETIMES____ NEVER____

4. How often do you stop chewing gum and put it in the garbage when you enter the classroom?

VERY OFTEN____ SOMETIMES____ NEVER____

5. How often do you go to your seat and get your books and papers ready before class starts?

VERY OFTEN____ SOMETIMES____ NEVER____

6. How often do you stop talking when the teacher signals attention?

VERY OFTEN____   SOMETIMES____   NEVER____

7. How often do you sit where you can actively take part in class discussions?

VERY OFTEN____   SOMETIMES____   NEVER____

8. How often do you try to be interested even when the class is boring?

VERY OFTEN____   SOMETIMES____   NEVER____

9. How often do you take notes in class?

VERY OFTEN____   SOMETIMES____   NEVER____

10. How often do you raise your hand and speak clearly when you're called on?

VERY OFTEN____   SOMETIMES____   NEVER____

11. How often do you really, *really*, REALLY listen to your teachers and the other students?

VERY OFTEN____   SOMETIMES____   NEVER____

12. How often do you get a good night's sleep before school?

VERY OFTEN____   SOMETIMES____   NEVER____

13. How often do you pay attention in class even if you know the material is not going to be on the next test?

VERY OFTEN____   SOMETIMES____   NEVER____

14. When you finish your work, how often do you find something quiet and useful to do?

VERY OFTEN____   SOMETIMES____   NEVER____

15. If you can't see or hear the teacher clearly, how often do you move to where you can instead of using that as an excuse?

VERY OFTEN____   SOMETIMES____   NEVER____

16. How often are you polite to teachers and other students?

VERY OFTEN____   SOMETIMES____   NEVER____

17. How often do you offer to help other students?

VERY OFTEN____   SOMETIMES____   NEVER____

18. How often do you clean up after yourself in class (straighten your desk, push your chair in, throw away stray papers)?

VERY OFTEN_____   SOMETIMES_____   NEVER_____

19. How often do you participate in class discussions?

VERY OFTEN_____   SOMETIMES_____   NEVER_____

20. How often do you eat a good breakfast so you're attentive, awake, and not hungry during school?

VERY OFTEN_____   SOMETIMES_____   NEVER_____

21. How often do you cooperate with the teacher's ideas and ways of teaching, even if you can't see the point?

VERY OFTEN_____   SOMETIMES_____   NEVER_____

22. How often do you volunteer for class activities?

VERY OFTEN_____   SOMETIMES_____   NEVER_____

23. How often do you volunteer for extracurricular activities?

VERY OFTEN_____   SOMETIMES_____   NEVER_____

24. How often are you quiet in the halls when other classes are in progress?

VERY OFTEN_____   SOMETIMES_____   NEVER_____

25. How often do you volunteer to do errands for the staff or the school secretaries?

VERY OFTEN_____   SOMETIMES_____   NEVER_____

26. How often do you do all of your homework or even more than is required?

VERY OFTEN_____   SOMETIMES_____   NEVER_____

27. How often do you take pride in your work and try to do your best job?

VERY OFTEN_____   SOMETIMES_____   NEVER_____

28. How often do you read books from the library?

VERY OFTEN_____   SOMETIMES_____   NEVER_____

29. How often do you ask for extra help when you need it?

VERY OFTEN_____   SOMETIMES_____   NEVER_____

30. How often do you pay attention until the very last minute of class and stay seated until class is dismissed?

VERY OFTEN____   SOMETIMES____   NEVER____

31. How often do you work on building your vocabulary by looking up words you don't know?

VERY OFTEN____   SOMETIMES____   NEVER____

32. How often do you thank the teacher for a lesson when you leave the classroom?

VERY OFTEN____   SOMETIMES____   NEVER____

33. How often do you tell the teacher when a topic was especially interesting to you?

VERY OFTEN____   SOMETIMES____   NEVER____

34. How often do you read news, science, computer, or other educational magazines?

VERY OFTEN____   SOMETIMES____   NEVER____

35. How often do you watch the evening news or read the daily newspaper?

VERY OFTEN____   SOMETIMES____   NEVER____

36. How often do you bring relevant or interesting materials (cartoons, books, articles) to show in class?

VERY OFTEN____   SOMETIMES____   NEVER____

37. How often are you respectful and friendly to your teachers in the halls?

VERY OFTEN____   SOMETIMES____   NEVER____

39. How often do you notice relationships between facts or ideas from different subject areas, or between school and "real life"?

VERY OFTEN____   SOMETIMES____   NEVER____

40. How often do you offer an opinion based on sound reasons, and explain your reasons for having that opinion?

VERY OFTEN____   SOMETIMES____   NEVER____

41. How often do you look for the assumptions behind what other people say or believe?

VERY OFTEN____   SOMETIMES____   NEVER____

42. How often do you recognize what your own biases are?

VERY OFTEN____ SOMETIMES____ NEVER____

43. How often do you actively work at developing your mind through reading?

VERY OFTEN____ SOMETIMES____ NEVER____

44. How often do you actively work at improving your memory?

VERY OFTEN____ SOMETIMES____ NEVER____

45. How often do you ask a question in class just because you're curious?

VERY OFTEN____ SOMETIMES____ NEVER____

TOTAL:

SCORING

Give yourself 3 points for each VERY OFTEN, 2 points for each SOMETIMES, and 1 point for each NEVER. Then add up your score.

• *If your score is 105–135,* you are probably an excellent student. You know how to think and how to study. You're comfortable in the classroom, and you recognize the value of learning.

• *If your score is 85–104,* you are probably a good student. Keep up the good work! Practice the thinking skills described on pages 62–63 anyway.

• *If your score is 65–84,* you may be an average student. You could probably improve by making an extra effort to practice the thinking skills described on pages 62–63.

• *If your score is 45–64,* you may be a poor student. You probably need to prepare more for class, participate more in class discussions, and show more respect for learning, your teachers, your fellow learners, and ultimately yourself.

ACTIVITY 17

Some thinking skills to practice

Practicing these skills will make you a better thinker—and probably a better student, too. Ask your teacher for help with any you don't understand. Try to come up with examples for each. Think of good times to practice these thinking skills.

- COLLECTING AND ORGANIZING INFORMATION

Identify sources of information. Use those sources to find information. Examine the information you find. Take the information that's useful or relevant to a project you are working on. Organize it in a meaningful way.

- CODING

Develop your own "shorthand" methods for summarizing, diagraming, recording, and presenting information.

- COMPARING

Examine two or more items (including ideas). Identify their similarities and differences.

- CLASSIFYING

Examine several items (including ideas). Then sort them into groups according to their similarities and differences.

- DECISION-MAKING

Choose among alternatives. Examine the beliefs, attitudes, and feelings which lie behind the choices you make. Evaluate the consequences of your choices.

- EVALUATING

Criticize, make judgments, or offer opinions based on specific principles.

- HYPOTHESIZING

Come up with a variety of possible explanations for things that have happened in the past, things that are happening in the present, and things that might happen in the future.

- IDENTIFYING ASSUMPTIONS

Learn to tell the difference between something you *know* to be true (from facts or observations), and something you *take for granted* to be true.

- IMAGINING

Use your inner resources to create, fantasize, or visualize experiences. Create detailed mental images.

- INTERPRETING

Describe an experience, then explain what it means.

- OBSERVING

Use your senses to collect information about your environment. Study objects or experiences in detail.

• ANALYZING AND SYNTHESIZING

Break down information and ideas into parts, then analyze each part. Bring together all information and ideas that are relevant to the topic, then organize them in a way that makes sense.

• PROBLEM-SOLVING

Identify and define a problem. Collect and organize information about it. Generate and test hypotheses about the nature and source of the problem. Suggest a variety of possible solutions, and predict their consequences. Develop an action plan, then try it. Evaluate the results of your problem-solving activities.

• SUMMARIZING AND CONDENSING

Examine a body of information. Try to figure out the "core meanings." Write the core meanings in as simple a way as you can — one or two sentences, or a short paragraph.

ACTIVITY 17

Fifteen tips for becoming a better listener

Being a good listener is a very important part of being a good student. Here are some tips for improving your listening skills.

1. Don't interrupt a speaker until he or she has finished talking.

2. Mentally block out distractions and concentrate.

3. Try to understand the speaker's point of view by putting yourself in his or her place.

4. Try to anticipate what comes next.

5. Look for hidden assumptions, biases, unsupported opinions, and generalizations.

6. Don't memorize every single fact the speaker mentions. Instead, try to remember the broader, more general ideas.

7. Try to visualize what's being said.

8. Take notes as the speaker talks. Write down key words and phrases, plus any questions you have along the way.

9. Ask questions if you don't understand something the speaker has said. Wait for an appropriate time.

10. Show interest in what is being said by your actions, gestures, and what you say in response.

11. Look for ideas or examples that are interesting to you, even when you think the topic is boring.

12. Try to think of examples of what's being explained or discussed.

13. Try to relate any new information or ideas to something you already know.

14. Repeat or summarize the main points of a lecture, lesson, or chapter at the end to make sure you have understood correctly.

15. Discuss what you heard with your classmates and your parents. Try to talk with someone who may give you more information on the topic, or help you understand it in a new way.

Three steps to becoming a better writer

START BY IDENTIFYING

A. What's the *purpose* of what you're writing? Put a check mark by one or more of these:

____ to narrate

____ to describe

____ to explain

____ to persuade

____ to entertain

____ to inform

____ to console

____ to celebrate

____ to denounce

____ to provoke

____ to question

____ to commemorate

____ to satirize

____ to comment on

____ other: _____

B. Who's the *audience* you're writing to? Put a check mark by one or more of these:

____ my family

____ my friend(s)

____ my classmates

____ my teacher

____ my employer

____ my mentor

____ my muse

____ myself

____ younger children

____ someone special

____ the general public

____ a special interest group

____ a different culture or society

____ the past

____ the future

____ other: _____

ACTIVITY 17

C. What's the *form* your writing is supposed to take? Put a check mark by one or more of these:

____ paragraph	____ summary
____ essay	____ recipe
____ short story	____ review (of a play, book, movie, or record)
____ letter	
____ monologue	____ news article
____ dialogue	____ song
____ speech	____ book report
____ script	____ biography
____ science fiction story	____ autobiography
____ tall tale	____ poem
____ myth	____ play
____ cartoon caption	____ journal or diary entry
____ outline	____ historical account
____ research paper	____ other: _____

MASTER THE WRITING PROCESS

Read and practice TOWARD EXCELLENT WORK to improve your writing.

T hink! Talk to others!

O utline ideas according to PURPOSE, AUDIENCE, and FORM (see Step 1, "Start By Identifying").

W rite a series of brief notes which develop your outline.

A nalyze your notes.

R esearch as required.

D raft your first copy.

E dit your first copy.

X TIME OUT: Let the copy sit for a while. Then start all over *or* draft a second copy.

C heck for content, coherence, consistencies, climax…

E mphasis, unity…

L iveliness, tone, and…

L anguage usage. Then…

E dit orally. Read it aloud to someone else.

N ow draft a third copy to correct any left-over stylistic and mechanical errors.

T est on a "trial reader."

W rite your final copy. Doublecheck…

O verall editing, and overall appearance.

R elease to readers.

K eep at least one copy for yourself.

Something to think about

Writing comes alive when you strive for five:

1. originality
2. clarity
3. unity
4. coherence
5. interest

Check these six mechanics' tricks:

1. capitalization
2. punctuation
3. spelling
4. grammar
5. format and appearance
6. overall editing

ACTIVITY 17

3

SHARE YOUR WORK

After you make at least one copy to keep for yourself, consider sharing your writing. Put a check mark by each idea you plan to try:

_____ read it aloud to family, friends, or a wider audience

_____ make another copy and give it to someone as a gift

_____ publish it in a newspaper, magazine, or journal

_____ display it on a class bulletin board

_____ record it on tape with music

_____ record it on tape with music, then make a slide show

_____ use it as a radio broadcast or play

_____ enter it in a contest

_____ give it to other teachers or classes to read

_____ illustrate it, or have a friend illustrate it

_____ illustrate it, then display it in a collection

_____ dedicate it to someone special

_____ send it to someone who lives in another city, country, or culture

_____ other: _____

Be a better reader with SQ3R

Use the SQ3R strategy to read more effectively and retain more of what you read.

S urvey the chapter, article, story, or other item to be read. Skim headings, subheadings, key words, and phrases.

Q uestion what you may find when you read the material in detail. Ask yourself what you expect to know when you have finished reading, and jot down a few of your questions.

R ead. Carefully and completely. If you think it will help, read aloud and underline key words and ideas as you read.

R ecite and repeat the key points you have learned after reading.

R eview. Come back in an hour, a day, or a week and repeat this process. Each time you do it, you'll be quicker at it. Eventually you'll just have to go over the key points you identified earlier.

ACTIVITY 18

WHAT'S YOUR LEARNING STYLE?

Explain in as much detail as you can how you would go about doing each of these tasks:

1. Build a shelf for your room

_____

_____

_____

_____

_____

_____

_____

2. Become a good guitar player

_____

_____

_____

_____

_____

_____

_____

3. Plan and prepare a balanced meal

_____

_____

_____

_____

_____

_____

4. Learn to spell twenty words correctly for a test

_____

_____

_____

_____

_____

_____

ACTIVITY 18

5. Write a report on a subject you don't know anything about

_____

_____

_____

_____

_____

_____

_____

6. Get a part-time job

_____

_____

_____

_____

_____

_____

_____

Your learning style

Over the years, you have probably developed at least one way of learning that seems to work best for you in most situations. This way of learning is your *learning style*. Or you may move from one learning style to another, depending on the learning task.

Read these descriptions of learning styles. Then go back and re-read your descriptions of how you would perform the six tasks (from building a shelf to getting a part-time job). Which learning style (or combination of learning styles) comes closest to your style in each case?

• *Tactile or kinesthetic learning* means learning through hands-on experience. Most people, regardless of their age, learn best when they can touch, move, sew, hammer, or write something themselves.

Infants and toddlers reach for and touch whatever objects are around them. Older children like to handle plastic, wooden, cloth, or cardboard numbers and letters as they begin to learn math and spelling.

Tactile learning is important in sports, the sciences, the arts, and vocational training (such as woodworking, fine welding, hairdressing, and computer operation).

• *Auditory learning* is learning by listening. Some people learn best when they are told what to do. These people need to hear an explanation or listen to a lecture.

• *Visual learning* is learning by looking. Some people learn most effectively when they see a demonstration or read words, charts, maps, or diagrams.

In school, auditory and visual learning often are combined. For example, you may see a film with narration. Or your teacher may explain a concept while drawing a diagram on the blackboard. Or you may be asked to respond out loud or in writing to something you have seen or read.

Tactile learners are at a disadvantage in school. The higher the grade level, the more the teacher depends on auditory instruction.

ACTIVITY 18

If you have trouble learning...

...and there is no apparent physical or psychological reason, you may have one or more *learning disabilities.* You may need to learn in special ways.

People with learning disabilities may be as smart as (or even smarter than) their peers. Often, they score above average on standardized intelligence tests. They just *learn differently.*

Learning disabilities may affect your ability to hear correctly or completely. They may make it difficult for you to see things the way most people do. They may even affect your sense of touch. You may feel uncoordinated at times. You may feel confused when you try to think about some things. It may be hard for you to focus attention on one thing at a time.

If you think you have a learning disability, a trained specialist can test you to identify the disability. Ask your parents, teacher, or school counselor to get the help you need to make learning easier for you.

Although you may have more trouble learning than other students do, you *can* learn ways to learn that work for you.

If you are academically gifted...

...learning in school may be so easy for you that you always do well. Or maybe you don't. Not all academically gifted students do well in school. Some do well some of the time, but not all of the time. And some don't do well at all.

Why do some academically gifted kids do poorly in school? Here are a few possible reasons:

• When the teacher asks you for the answer to question 3, you may respond incorrectly because you are already working on question 33.

• Maybe you're so bored by assignments that are too easy for you, or by working with kids who don't catch on as quickly as you do, that you don't even bother doing your work.

• The other kids may make fun of you because the things that interest you don't interest them. You may become depressed or angry and decide not to apply yourself in school. Or you may decide to do less than your best so you'll "fit in" with the other kids.

• Your parents and teachers may have such high expectations of you that you can't possibly succeed. Or you may have too-high expectations of yourself.

Being gifted can sometimes make it hard for you to see things the way most people do. You may see problems and solutions where others don't. You may be very upset about serious social problems like famine, pollution, and war while others don't seem to be affected as strongly, or at all. You may feel lonely and isolated, frustrated and misunderstood.

If you are academically gifted, it's important for you to spend a part of your school time being challenged by gifted peers and teachers who will help and encourage you. Ask your parents, teacher, or school counselor to help you get the help you need. Meanwhile, try to learn as much as you can in your current situation.

Something to think about

Do you think globally *(in large, interrelated chunks)? Or do you think* sequentially *(in logical units, one idea or fact after another)? Can you switch back and forth between these two ways of thinking whenever you want to, or when circumstances make it necessary?*

ACTIVITY 19

TIME MANAGEMENT

Many students say they have too much to do —
too much homework, too many extracurricular activities, too many
tests, too many classes.

Time management skills can help you organize your time and make
the most of it. It can help you feel less stressed and more in control of
your life.

Use the chart on the next page to record your activities for one
week. At the end of the week, look it over. Are there blocks of time you
can use more effectively?

Keep using this chart for a month or two to get an even better
picture of how you spend your time. Then make adjustments, if
necessary, to be sure that you control time, and that time doesn't
control you.

ACTIVITY 19

MY TIME MANAGEMENT

	Monday	Tuesday	Wednesday	Thursday	Friday	Saturday	Sunday
6:00–7:00 AM							
7:00–8:00							
8:00–9:00							
9:00–10:00							
10:00–11:00							
11:00–12:00 N							
12:00–1:00 PM							
1:00–2:00							
2:00–3:00							
3:00–4:00							
4:00–5:00							
5:00–6:00							
6:00–7:00							
7:00–8:00							
8:00–9:00							
9:00–10:00							
10:00–11:00							
11:00–12:00 M							

77

STUDY STRATEGIES

If you want to be a better student, consider trying some new study strategies. Read each of these suggestions. Put a star beside the ones you already do. Put a check mark by the ones you're willing to try. Then do them *every day* for the next two weeks.

____ 1. Before you leave school for the day, make sure that you understand what you're supposed to do for each assignment. If you don't understand, ask.

____ 2. Set up a regular homework schedule, with regular breaks to reward yourself. Stick to the schedule for one week, then revise it if necessary.

____ 3. Gather everything you need to do your homework (such as pens, pencils, erasers, dictionary, calculator, and paper) in one place. Use that place only for studying.

____ 4. Follow directions exactly.

____ 5. Make lists of the things you must do and the order you will do them in.

____ 6. Do your hardest assignments first, when you are fresh and have the most energy. Or alternate between easy and hard assignments.

____ 7. Reread your class notes at the end of each day. Expand them and highlight key concepts to make future reviews easier. Review them again before the week is over. Can you make any improvements in the way you take notes or organize your notebook?

____ 8. Read, review, and study early in the morning, or at some other time when you can be alone and work without interruption.

____ 9. Don't take phone calls during your study time. Tell your friends not to call because you are studying at that specific time.

____ 10. Don't watch TV while you're studying. If you usually listen to music, try studying without it. Or, if you don't usually listen to music, try studying with it for a change.

____ 11. Practice reading at different speeds. Some material may require you to read slowly and carefully. For easier material, or material you are already familiar with, try skimming.

____ 12. If you usually study with a friend, study alone. If you usually study alone, try studying with a friend.

____ 13. Find a tutor to work with. In some cases, you may not have to pay him or her. (For example, your school may have a peer tutoring program. Or maybe you can arrange to do his or her chores in exchange for tutoring.)

____ 14. Organize your time so you can complete chores and other activities before you begin your homework. Have a snack, go to the bathroom, and make necessary phone calls before you sit down to work.

____ 15. Take periodic breaks — but limit them, and return to work soon.

____ 16. Talk to yourself. Read your written answers out loud to make sure they answer the questions and sound sensible. Repeat concepts out loud as you read. Give yourself verbal encouragement by saying things like "You're doing fine," "You're getting the idea," "You're almost finished," and so on.

____ 17. Have fun making up memory aids (called *mnemonics*) using the initials of words you must remember. For example: For the colors of the spectrum — Red, Orange, Yellow, Green, Blue, Indigo, and Violet — remember the man's name ROY G. BIV. For becoming a better writer, remember TOWARD EXCELLENT WORK (see page 67).

____ 18. Keep an updated list for each subject of difficult vocabulary words, formulas, or concepts. Keep the list current by crossing out the items you've mastered and adding new ones that you need to learn.

____ 19. Try to do more than the bare minimum that's required. For example, read some of the other material your teacher suggests, or do some library research of your own. Your interest in a subject will soar, and so will your grades.

____ 20. Try to prepare for your classes ahead of time. Read in advance material that your teacher will be presenting. Often what you thought might be a boring class will turn out to be fun when you can anticipate what will happen next.

____ 21. Don't let yourself fall behind. Complete all of your assignments on time. If you fall behind anyway (due to illness or some other problem), take a closer look at your schedule and make adjustments. Maybe you need to complete assignments earlier than their due dates.

ACTIVITY 21

BE SURE TO FOLLOW DIRECTIONS!

How good are you at following directions? Find out by doing this simple exercise.

NAME: _____ GRADE: _____ DATE: _____

1. Read everything before you do anything.

2. Put your name in the upper right-hand corner of this page.

3. Circle the word "name" in step #2.

4. Draw five small squares in the upper left-hand corner.

5. Write an "X" in each of the squares you drew in the upper left-hand corner.

6. Sign your name under the heading, "Activity 21," at the top of this page.

7. Then write, "It's Important To Follow Directions."

8. Draw a circle around step #7.

9. Write an "X" in the lower left-hand corner of this page and draw a circle around it.

10. Multiply 70 by 30 and write the answer here:_____.

11. Draw a circle around the word "page" in step #6.

12. Call out your first name so everyone can hear it.

13. Add 107 and 234 and write your answer here: _____. Now circle your answer.

14. If you have followed each direction so far, call out, "I have followed all the directions."

15. Underline all the even numbers in this set of directions.

16. Count backwards, out loud, from 10 to 1.

17. Do only what is asked of you in step 2. Then sit quietly and wait for everyone else to show you how good they are at following directions.

What did you just learn about following directions? How will this help you the next time you have to take a test?

TEST-TAKING TIPS

Teachers use tests to find out how fast and how thoroughly you learn in school. Before taking a test, you must study and review the material to be tested. You must also know the proper way to take a test. How you handle the test-taking situation can affect your performance and ultimately your grade.

Read these test-taking suggestions. Check YES for the ones you DO think sound helpful. Check NO for the ones you think DON'T sound helpful.

	YES	NO
1. Arrive on time.	☐	☐
2. Forget your pencils and pens.	☐	☐
3. Look through the test to make sure no pages or sections are missing.	☐	☐
4. Start right in with the first question.	☐	☐
5. Do the hardest questions first.	☐	☐
6. Hurry! Then leave as soon as you are finished.	☐	☐
7. Watch what your neighbor is doing.	☐	☐
8. Take some deep breaths before you start. Shake your arms and hands. Loosen up.	☐	☐
9. Ask the teacher to explain any question you don't understand.	☐	☐
10. Poke along, taking as much time as you want for each question.	☐	☐
11. Check your paper over before you hand it in.	☐	☐
12. In an essay test, number each answer properly so it's clear which questions each refers to.	☐	☐

	YES	NO
13. Budget your time. Consider the value of the question in deciding how long you will spend on it and how detailed your answer will be.	☐	☐
14. Don't list key concepts or dates on a piece of scrap paper before you begin your test. You probably won't need them.	☐	☐
15. Refuse to accept your anxiety as a natural feeling in a test situation. Fight it.	☐	☐
16. The day before the exam, make up a practice test filled with questions you think you might be asked.	☐	☐
17. Go to an exam well rested, calm, and prepared.	☐	☐
18. If you are allowed to write on the test paper, underline key words in the directions and questions.	☐	☐
19. Daydream and pretend you're somewhere else.	☐	☐
20. Think positive. Do your best. Give a great performance!	☐	☐

Something to think about

- *If the test doesn't ask about anything you know, should you write down everything you do know rather than turn in a blank paper?*

- *Try thinking of tests as challenges rather than obstacles.*

ACTIVITY 22

ANSWERS

Here are the best responses to each test-taking tip:

1. Yes. Being late puts you at a disadvantage before you start.

2. No. Bring at least two of each, plus a ruler and an eraser.

3. Yes. If you get a paper with errors on it, ask for a correct one right away. Ask for scrap paper, too (see tip #14).

4. No. Look through the whole test first and budget your time (see tip #13). This will also give you a chance to find questions that are closely related so answering one helps you to answer the other(s).

5. It depends. You may want to get them out of the way so you can relax, or you may want to do the easy ones first to build your confidence.

6. No. Take your time. If you have extra time, look over the test again. Do the hard questions over again just to be sure of your answers. Expand your answers by including more facts or examples.

7. No. Do your own work.

8. Yes. Increased blood flow takes more oxygen to your brain so it works better.

9. Yes. Perhaps the teacher can give you a clue. Then again, the teacher might say, "You're on your own!"

10. No. Pace yourself.

11. Yes. You may have missed something.

12. Yes. Helping the teacher (or other person who marks your test) with organization and neatness may improve your grade.

13. Yes. See #10.

14. No. As soon as the test begins, jot down important diagrams, formulas, concepts, or dates on a separate sheet of paper. Otherwise you may forget them.

15. No. Just relax and do your best.

16. Yes. Anticipating what will be asked helps you to identify the important concepts.

17. Yes. Don't stay up late studying, especially if you're not a morning person.

18. Yes. Sometimes a clue to an earlier question appears later in the test.

19. No. Mentally block out distractions and keep focused on the test.

20. Yes. Do well so you can be proud of yourself. Perform! Strut your stuff! *Show* what you *know!*

YOUR I.Q.

Every person has certain information, attitudes, and ideas that he or she has gained through experience and insight. Together, these are called *general knowledge* and *common sense.*

Schools try to identify how much you know, how well you think, and your potential for learning by giving you standardized tests. Your score on a standardized intelligence test is called your *intelligence quotient*, or *I.Q.*

On most intelligence tests, if your score is the same as most students your age, your I.Q. will be 100. If your score is higher than that of most students your age, your I.Q. will be over 100. If your score is less than that of most students your age, your I.Q. will be less than 100.

Even though psychologists have designed tests to measure intelligence, they can't agree on what intelligence is. Many psychologists argue that standardized tests don't accurately test students because they don't test creative ability in literature, music, art, or problem solving. Others say the tests shouldn't be the same for everyone because people differ in their cultural backgrounds, economic opportunities, values, and other social factors. Because these factors affect people's ability to *perceive* (observe), learn, *infer* (solve), and *retain* (remember) information and ideas, giving the same test to everyone isn't fair, some psychologists say. They claim the tests are *biased*, or slanted, in favor of students from certain ethnic and economic groups — usually the same groups as those the test-makers belong to.

Still others say that an I.Q. score is an artificial number that may have very little to do with how smart you really are. If you were ill the day you took the test, if you had trouble reading the questions, or if the test didn't ask about things you know, your score wouldn't be an accurate measure of your abilities.

Until psychologists come up with a better way of testing students, however, educators will probably keep using standardized intelligence tests.

ACTIVITY 23

Once you have taken one of these tests, your teachers may expect you to perform according to your I.Q. If your I.Q. is high, they may expect you to perform very well. If your I.Q. is average or lower, they may not expect much of you.

Psychologists have found that teachers' expectations can make a big difference in how well students learn. In one famous experiment, which has been repeated several times in different schools and classes, teachers were assigned to teach "honors" classes. The teachers were told that the classes were made up of very bright children. In fact, they were made up of average children. By the end of the term, however, many of the students were doing exceptionally well. Because the teachers expected them to excel, they did. This is called the *halo effect*.

1

Have you ever taken a standardized intelligence test, a series of ability tests, or a creativity test? YES ☐ NO ☐

If YES, what do you remember about it?

_____

_____

2

Do you think that any single test can really measure someone's intelligence? YES ☐ NO ☐

If NO, what do you think would be a better way to measure intelligence?

_____

_____

3

Do you know your I.Q.? YES ☐ NO ☐

If NO, answer these questions. (If YES, move on to question #4.)

• Imagine that you've just learned your I.Q. It's 174 — you're a genius! How does this make you feel?

_____

_____

How do you think this will affect your school performance?

_____

_____

How do you think this will affect your dreams and plans?

_____

_____

• Imagine that you've just learned your I.Q. It's 100 — you're *exactly* average. How does this make you feel?

_____

_____

How do you think this will affect your school performance?

_____

_____

How do you think this will affect your dreams and plans?

_____

_____

• Imagine that you've just learned your I.Q. It's 130 — but everybody in your family and all of your friends score in the 150+ range. How does this make you feel?

_____

_____

How do you think this will affect your school performance?

_____

_____

How do you think this will affect your future?

_____

_____

• Imagine that you've just learned your I.Q. It's 73 — well *below* average. How does this make you feel?

_____

_____

How do you think this will affect your school performance?

_____

_____

How do you think this will affect your future?

_____

_____

Some experts think that it's not a good idea for young people to know their I.Q. If it's high, they feel pressured to perform. If it's low, they lower their expectations of themselves. What's your opinion?

_____

_____

If you know your I.Q., would you say that this information has helped you or hurt you? Why?

_____

_____

Intelligence has been defined as "what you do when you don't know what to do." Do you agree with this definition? YES ☐ NO ☐

Explain your answer:

_____

_____

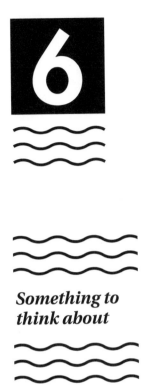

Something to think about

How important is your I.Q. to how you live your daily life?
☐ VERY IMPORTANT ☐ KIND OF IMPORTANT ☐ NOT VERY IMPORTANT ☐ NOT IMPORTANT AT ALL

Explain your answer:

_____

_____

_____

If you don't know your I.Q. and you'd like to know it, this information may be in your school's files. Legally, you and/or your parents have the right to know your standardized test scores. If you are interested, find out the procedure at your school. But be sure to think about this first. Do you really want to know your I.Q.? What if it's higher than you think it should be? What if it's lower? Will this affect your self-image and your expectations of yourself?

ACTIVITY 24

IMPROVING YOUR INTELLECTUAL PERFORMANCE

Do you think you can be smarter? Maybe, maybe not. But you *can* learn more and discover more every day, if you choose to.

Many people improve their intellectual performance by improving their reading, researching, observing, and listening habits and skills. They take good care of their physical health. They write down ideas they have or interesting things they learn. They meditate to clear their minds and make room for new thoughts. They use their imaginations. They strive to develop their memories. They constantly set intellectual challenges for themselves — *and so can you.*

What are some things you can do to improve your intellectual performance? List as many as you can think of.

_____

_____

_____

_____

_____

_____

_____

Now pick three things from your list. Do them for at least one week. What improvements do you notice in the quality of your life?

_____

_____

_____

_____

Do you think you have become more intelligent, or are you just making better use of the intelligence you have always had?

_____

_____

_____

_____

_____

INTELLIGENCE ISN'T ENOUGH

To succeed in school, you need more than brains alone. Some of the other things you need are shown on the chart on the next page. Put a check mark under "good," "average," or "poor" to rate your own intelligence, health, attitude toward school, and so on. Then think about how much each one is affecting your current academic performance. Put a check mark under "not at all," "some," or "a lot."

ACTIVITY 25

	good	average	poor	How much does this affect your academic performance?		
				not at all	some	a lot
your intelligence						
your general health						
your eating habits						
your sleeping habits						
how much TV you watch						
your attitude toward school						
how much effort you make in school						
your school attendance						
your personality						
luck						
how much money your family has						
how stable your family is						
how much support your family gives you						
your peer group						
your short-range plans						
your long-range plans						

ACTIVITY 26

EXTRACURRICULAR ACTIVITIES

extracurricular *(adj.) 1. of or relating to organized student activities that usually carry no academic credit 2. lying outside one's regular duties or routine.*

The debate team, the school play, computer club, swimming, music, dance lessons, sports teams — these are all extracurricular activities. By joining one or more, you expand your formal education AND you meet other people who share your interests. You have new experiences and learn new skills.

Extracurricular activities can help you live a fuller, more interesting school life. This in turn can give you more choices in adult life and a better understanding of the world.

1. List the extracurricular activities at your school that you COULD participate in:

____ _____

____ _____

____ _____

____ _____

____ _____

____ _____

____ _____

____ _____

____ _____

2. Now put a star by each one that you DO participate in.

3. Put a check mark by each extracurricular activity that you WANT TO participate in, but haven't yet tried.

4. Pick one or two, then experience them if you can.

5. If you don't want to participate in any extracurricular activities, why not? Write an explanation that satisfies YOU:

_____

_____

_____

ACTIVITY 27

READ!

One of the best and least expensive ways to learn more about the world is to *read*. From magazines, newspapers, and books, you can find out how things work and how people in different cultures live. You can read a scary story or a beautiful poem. You can travel anywhere in the world or find out more about yourself. And public libraries are free! All you need is a library card.

If you are vision impaired, you can still read. Libraries have cassette tapes of people reading a wide variety of books. You might enjoy listening to these.

Nonfiction books are full of facts, but that doesn't mean they are boring. An *autobiography* of a famous baseball player or rock star is an example of a nonfiction book you might find interesting. (An autobiography is a person's life story, told by himself or herself.) Other nonfiction books might be about wild animals, race car engines, and careers. Books have been written on everything you're interested in.

Fiction books are written from the author's imagination. Novels, poetry, and short stories are usually works of fiction. Your librarian can show you the fiction and nonfiction areas of your library.

1. What is your favorite nonfiction book?

TITLE: _____

AUTHOR: _____

2. What is your favorite fiction book?

TITLE: _____

AUTHOR: _____

Would you like some suggestions about what to read? Ask around. Your parents, teachers, librarian, brothers and sisters, friends, and neighbors have favorite books they'll be glad to tell you about. List them here, and write the name of the person who recommended each one. The next time you're at the library, look for some of these books. Read them, discuss them with the people who recommended them to you, and recommend them to other people.

TITLE: _____

AUTHOR: _____

PERSON RECOMMENDING THIS BOOK: _____

DATE READ: _____

TITLE: _____

AUTHOR: _____

PERSON RECOMMENDING THIS BOOK: _____

DATE READ: _____

TITLE: _____

AUTHOR: _____

PERSON RECOMMENDING THIS BOOK: _____

DATE READ: _____

ACTIVITY 27

TITLE: _____

AUTHOR: _____

PERSON RECOMMENDING THIS BOOK: _____

DATE READ: _____

TITLE: _____

AUTHOR: _____

PERSON RECOMMENDING THIS BOOK: _____

DATE READ: _____

JUST FOR FUN: Ask the librarian if there are records, films, maps, or other special kinds of material in the library that are not out on the shelves. Ask to see the front page of the newspaper on the day you were born! The librarian may be able to give you a laminated copy, enlarged from the microfilm or microfiche, to hang in your room. This would also make a great inexpensive birthday gift. Another gift idea: Read a story, a whole book, or some poems onto a cassette tape. Pick things you think the other person will enjoy listening to.

Something to think about

Censorship *is when one person or group stops other people from reading, seeing, or listening to something labeled "objectionable" or "inappropriate." Over time, many books have been censored. People haven't been allowed to print them, sell them, buy them, or read them. Some movies and radio programs are censored for certain age groups.*

Does censorship affect what you are allowed to read, watch, or listen to? Do you think censorship is a good idea? Do you think that authors, artists, and musicians should be allowed to say, show, or sing anything to anyone at any time?

MUSIC, MUSIC, MUSIC

Music is all around us: on the radio and on TV, in stores and elevators, in cars and on the street. Like many things, music becomes more enjoyable when you know more about it. You may be learning about music in school, or you may take music lessons, but you can educate *yourself* by listening to a wide variety of composers, musicians, and types of music.

Over the next few weeks, try to listen to at least one example of each of the types of music listed in the chart on the next page. Your parents may have records or tapes you can borrow. Your school library may loan out records and tapes. Your public library probably has a large collection of music people can check out and listen to at home.

If you're not sure where to start, ask your family, teachers, friends, or neighbors for suggestions. If some of the music types aren't familiar to you, ask someone to tell you about them or to recommend albums or selections. If you discover other types of music you want to listen to, add them to the chart.

For each type you listen to, list the title of the album or selection, the name(s) of the composer(s) (a composer is a person who writes music), the performer or group, and the date you listened. Then rate the album or selection according to how much you liked it. Use a scale of 1 to 10, with 10 being something you liked very much and 1 being something you disliked very much.

If you are hearing impaired, you can still learn about music. Ask your teacher to arrange a visit to a music store or a band performance so you can see and handle many different kinds of musical instruments. Feel the vibrations of the various kinds of musical rhythms. Have your classmates "act out" how each kind of music makes them feel, or have them demonstrate each rhythm. Watch dancers dance to each type of music, then design a dance of your own to the music you hear inside yourself and perform it for your friends. Or work with them to stage a dance performance to a piece of music — you can choreograph their movements to the beat, rhythm, and emotions they describe, paint the sets, or sew the costumes.

ACTIVITY 28

Type	Title	Composer(s)	Performer or group	Rating	Date
instrumental					
vocal					
madrigal					
waltz					
electronic					
chamber music					
symphony					
reggae					
jazz					
blues					
R&B (rhythm and blues)					
ethnic (or "world music")					
rock					
rap					
folk					
pop					
gospel					
classical					
religious					
country					
big band					
march					
concerto					
ballad					
new age (or "space music")					
_____					

SEEING IS LEARNING: OBSERVE!

Still another way to educate yourself is by keeping your eyes open. You learn by looking at things — some of which may be beautiful, some of which may be ugly, all of which are interesting. You learn by looking at art and architecture, crafts, nature, athletic events, fashions, TV and movies, shapes, colors, and textures. You learn by looking upside down, close up, and from unusual angles.

Which of the things listed here have you seen with your own eyes, in person or in pictures? Which would you like to see someday? (Add your own ideas to the end of the list.)

If you are vision impaired, you can still "see." Ask someone to help you touch, smell, taste, or otherwise experience these things, or to describe them to you. Your friends may want to take a test you design for them: Put a dozen items on a tray and see if they can identify them while blindfolded. (If your friends prepare a tray for you, do you think you will do better or worse than they do at identifying the objects?)

ACTIVITY 29

Item	Have seen with my own eyes	Would like to see with my own eyes someday
a cartoon film	☐	☐
embroidery	☐	☐
the Eiffel Tower	☐	☐
a rainbow	☐	☐
Michelangelo's Sistine Chapel	☐	☐
a flower arrangement	☐	☐
a modern dance performance	☐	☐
a kaleidoscope	☐	☐
a honeycomb	☐	☐
the inside of a pomegranate	☐	☐
a large neon sign	☐	☐
a wax seal	☐	☐
a stained glass window	☐	☐
a rock video	☐	☐
a foreign film with subtitles	☐	☐
Leonardo da Vinci's Mona Lisa	☐	☐
a movie set in a different country	☐	☐
a waterfall	☐	☐
a TV program about nature	☐	☐
a patchwork quilt	☐	☐
a detective show	☐	☐
an Impressionist painting	☐	☐
a news documentary	☐	☐
The Leaning Tower of Pisa	☐	☐
an art museum	☐	☐
London's Big Ben	☐	☐
a play	☐	☐
the Taj Mahal	☐	☐
a musical	☐	☐
a collage	☐	☐
a balcony	☐	☐

Item	Have seen with my own eyes	Would like to see with my own eyes someday
a light show	☐	☐
someone making jewelry	☐	☐
a metal sculpture	☐	☐
a lace doily	☐	☐
hairstyling	☐	☐
the Acropolis	☐	☐
hand lettering	☐	☐
a batik scarf	☐	☐
a political cartoon	☐	☐
a piñata	☐	☐
an art-glass object	☐	☐
decals	☐	☐
a video game	☐	☐
folk costumes from other countries	☐	☐
a photo of the moon, or a photo of Earth from space	☐	☐
a tattoo	☐	☐
a marble or granite statue	☐	☐
weaving	☐	☐
a sculpture made of wood	☐	☐
a hologram	☐	☐
basket making	☐	☐
leather tooling	☐	☐
an English garden	☐	☐
a spire, steeple, or turret	☐	☐
a wrought-iron fence	☐	☐
a painting or print by a Native American artist	☐	☐
cut-outs by Matisse	☐	☐
ceramics/pottery	☐	☐
Michelangelo's David	☐	☐

ACTIVITY 29

Item	Have seen with my own eyes	Would like to see with my own eyes someday
a gymnastics performance	☐	☐
a landscape	☐	☐
a fountain	☐	☐
a sunset	☐	☐
wallpaper	☐	☐
a fire escape	☐	☐
an indoor sculpture	☐	☐
a surrealistic painting	☐	☐
a silhouette	☐	☐
a portrait	☐	☐
calligraphy	☐	☐
a profile	☐	☐
an abstract painting	☐	☐
a wildlife painting by Robert Bateman	☐	☐
an extreme close-up photograph	☐	☐
a work by Georgia O'Keeffe	☐	☐
a wide-angle photograph	☐	☐
a garden	☐	☐
a war photograph	☐	☐
a totem pole	☐	☐
a painting by Rembrandt	☐	☐
a billboard	☐	☐
a ballet	☐	☐
a map of the constellations	☐	☐
a decorative fan or screen	☐	☐
the Pyramids in Egypt	☐	☐
a bridge	☐	☐
a train trestle	☐	☐
a mask	☐	☐
a spider web	☐	☐
a maze	☐	☐

Item	Have seen with my own eyes	Would like to see with my own eyes someday
an ethnic costume	☐	☐
an asymmetrical shape	☐	☐
a beautiful door or gate	☐	☐
an interesting chimney	☐	☐
an aerial photograph	☐	☐
a monochrome (single-color) painting	☐	☐
velvet	☐	☐
satin	☐	☐
corduroy	☐	☐
a painting by Picasso	☐	☐
the Great Wall of China	☐	☐
someone shaping metal in a forge	☐	☐
Disney World	☐	☐
Ukrainian Easter eggs	☐	☐
a flowering tree in full bloom	☐	☐
the Statue of Liberty	☐	☐
_____	☐	☐
_____	☐	☐
_____	☐	☐
_____	☐	☐
_____	☐	☐

Something to think about

Watching TV with the sound off is the opposite of listening to the radio. Try it! This activity will help you learn to be more observant because the dialogue and sound track no longer direct your attention. You are free to look — and really see.

ACTIVITY 30

MORE WAYS TO EDUCATE YOURSELF

In *You and School,* you've learned some ways to improve your intellectual performance and to educate yourself. Can you think of other ways to educate yourself? Come up with as many as you can and list them here.

____ _____

____ _____

____ _____

____ _____

____ _____

____ _____

____ _____

____ _____

____ _____

____ _____

Now put a check mark by each one you think you'll try sometime soon.

A good way to learn is to teach someone else. Can you think of ways you can educate others? Come up with as many as you can and list them here.

___ _____

___ _____

___ _____

___ _____

___ _____

___ _____

___ _____

___ _____

___ _____

___ _____

Now put a check mark by each one you think you'll try sometime soon.

ACTIVITY 30

Did you think of these?

How many of these ways to educate yourself did you think of?

- read, read, read, read, read...
- learn a new sport
- take an academic summer school or correspondence course
- train yourself to be a better listener
- make new friends, or a wider variety of friends
- travel
- explore parks and recreation programs in your area
- volunteer at a nursing home, hospital, day care center, or animal shelter
- take lessons in arts and crafts, music, foreign language, or other areas that interest you (trade lessons for work?)
- start a new hobby
- attend a variety of churches, synagogues, mosques, or non-denominational meetings
- go on a student exchange program
- get a pen pal
- talk to adults about current events, their work, their opinions, and their experiences
- get a book from the library on how to improve your writing vocabulary and skills
- watch a broader range of TV programs than you usually do; listen to a wider variety of music
- take a new route to school, and try to increase your powers of observation
- go to camp
- find out what public lectures are being given in your area, and go to one or more (most are free)
- subscribe to a newspaper or a magazine
- ask for books or tickets to cultural events (a play, a symphony) for your birthday

How many of these ways to educate others did you think of?

• read aloud something you have written, something that means a lot to you, or something you find interesting

• keep a journal for someone else in which you record what you learned, read, thought, or discussed with others each day

• take photographs or make a cassette recording about things that are interesting to you, then share your photos or recording with another person

• show someone how to do something you can do

• discuss a news item, a movie, a book, or an idea with one other person or a group

• design a survey or research project, or build or make something; share your methods and information with someone else

• offer to tutor another person

• read your own list of ways to educate yourself, plus the "Did you think of these?" list, then pick one or two to try with someone else…and help each other learn

YOUR NOTES AND THOUGHTS

MORE FREE SPIRIT BOOKS

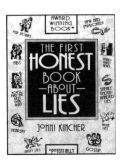

_____

_____

_____

Place
Stamp
Here

FREE SPIRIT PUBLISHING
400 FIRST AVENUE NORTH, SUITE 616
MINNEAPOLIS, MN 55401-1724

Free Spirit
PUBLISHING®

400 First Avenue North
Suite 616
Minneapolis, MN 55401-1724

612/338-2068
FAX 612/337-5050

**ORDER TOLL-FREE
1-800-735-7323**
Monday thru Friday
8:00 A.M.–5:00 P.M. CST

1 ☐ **PLEASE SEND ME THE FREE SPIRIT CATALOG**

2 NAME AND ADDRESS

NAME _____

ADDRESS _____

_____

CITY/STATE _____ ZIP ☐☐☐☐☐

3 SHIP TO (if different from billing address)

NAME _____

ADDRESS _____

CITY/STATE _____ ZIP ☐☐☐☐☐

4 DAYTIME TELEPHONE _____ (in case we have any questions)

5

TITLE	PRICE	QTY.	TOTAL

6 TOTAL

TO RECEIVE A FREE COPY OF THE FREE SPIRIT CATALOG, OR TO OBTAIN FREE SPIRIT PUBLICATIONS, PLEASE COMPLETE THIS FORM, ORDER BY TELEPHONE (1-800-735-7323) OR ASK FOR FREE SPIRIT BOOKS AT YOUR LOCAL BOOKSTORE.

SHIPPING & HANDLING

For merchandise
totals of:.......................Add:
Up to $10.00 ....$3.00
$10.01–$19.99...........$4.00
$20.00–$39.99...........$4.75
$40.00–$59.99...........$6.00
$60.00–$79.99...........$7.50
$80.00–$99.99...........$9.00
$100.00–$149.99....$10.00
$150 or more...............exact
shipping charges

Orders outside continental
North America **add**
$15.00 AIR MAIL

7 SUBTOTAL _____

8 SALES TAX
(6.5% MN ONLY) **+** _____

9 SHIPPING
& HANDLING **+** _____

10 TOTAL **$** _____

METHOD OF PAYMENT

☐ CHECK ☐ P.O. ATTACHED ☐ VISA ☐ MASTERCARD GOOD THROUGH ☐☐ — ☐☐

ACCOUNT # ☐☐☐☐☐☐☐☐☐☐☐☐☐☐☐☐

SIGNATURE _____

THANK YOU FOR YOUR ORDER!

SEND TO: Free Spirit Publishing Inc., 400 First Ave. North, Suite 616, Minneapolis MN 55401-1724

OR CALL: 1-800-735-7323
LOCAL: 612-338-2068, **FAX:** 612-337-5050

We offer discounts for quantity purchases.
Write or call for more information.